GETTING TO KNOW
THE U.S. PRESIDENTS

THOMAS
JEFFERSON

THIRD PRESIDENT
1801 – 1809

WRITTEN AND ILLUSTRATED BY MIKE VENEZIA

CHILDREN'S PRESS®
A DIVISION OF SCHOLASTIC INC.
NEW YORK   TORONTO   LONDON   AUCKLAND   SYDNEY
MEXICO CITY   NEW DELHI   HONG KONG
DANBURY, CONNECTICUT

Reading Consultant: Nanci R. Vargus, Ed.D., Assistant Professor, School of Education, University of Indianapolis

Historical Consultant: Marc J. Selverstone, Ph.D., Assistant Professor, Miller Center of Public Affairs, University of Virginia

Photographs © 2004:
Bridgeman Art Library International Ltd., London/New York: 16 (Blickling Hall, Norfolk, UK, National Trust Photographic Library/Christopher Hurst), 3, 25 right (New-York Historical Society, New York, USA)
Brown Brothers: 4
Corbis Images: 27 (AFP/Chicago Historical Society), 24 (Archivo Iconografico, S.A.), 9, 14, 30 (Bettmann), 11
North Wind Picture Archives: 28, 31 bottom, 31 top
Robertstock.com/R. Gilbert: 5
Steve Wolowina: 26
Superstock, Inc.: 20 (Stock Montage), 25 left (The Huntington Library, Art Collections, and Botanical Gardens, San Marino, CA), 19, 32

Colorist for illustrations: Dave Ludwig

Library of Congress Cataloging-in-Publication Data

Venezia, Mike.
    Thomas Jefferson / written and illustrated by Mike Venezia.
        p. cm.—(Getting to know the U.S. presidents)
Summary: An introduction to the life of Thomas Jefferson, a man whose ideas helped create a new kind of government and who became the nation's third president.
    ISBN 0-516-22608-8 (lib. bdg.)   0-516-27477-5 (pbk.)
    1. Jefferson, Thomas, 1743-1826—Juvenile literature. 2. Presidents—United States—Biography—Juvenile literature. [1. Jefferson, Thomas, 1743-1826. 2. Presidents.] I. Title.
    E332.79.V46 2004
    973.4'6'092—dc21

                    2003000009

4 5 6 7 8 9 10 R 13 12 11 10 09 08

A portrait of Thomas Jefferson by Rembrandt Peale (New-York Historical Society, New York)

Thomas Jefferson was the third president of the United States of America. He was born on his family's plantation in the colony of Virginia in 1743. Thomas Jefferson is best known for his intelligent and important ideas.

This is Thomas Jefferson's first drawing for the home he built at Monticello.

Thomas Jefferson believed ideas were the most powerful tools people could use. By thinking hard and coming up with good ideas, Thomas Jefferson invented ways to grow better fruits and vegetables on his plantation. He also designed a beautiful house all by himself.

Thomas built his house in an area he called Monticello, which in Italian means "little mountain." Everyone who saw Monticello admired it.

Most importantly, Thomas Jefferson's ideas helped create a new kind of government. This government cared about people's freedom and their right to do what they want with their lives.

Thomas Jefferson's home at Monticello

A government that cared about people's rights was unheard of during Thomas Jefferson's time. Throughout history, kings, queens, czars, and emperors had usually made the decisions about how people would live their lives.

When Thomas Jefferson was growing up, Virginia was a colony owned by England. The king of England at that time was George II. He got along pretty well with the people of the thirteen colonies in North America. It wasn't until later, when his grandson George III took over, that problems began.

The large plantation that Thomas Jefferson grew up on was called Shadwell. Most people who owned plantations had names for them. Thomas's father grew tobacco and other crops on his land. Mr. Jefferson was happy to teach his curious son all about farming. Thomas also learned how to build barns, stables, and storage sheds.

An engraving showing Cherokee leader Outacite

Thomas Jefferson was most interested in learning how to survey. He loved going out into the wilderness to map out and locate the boundaries of his family's land. Out in the wilderness, Thomas studied nature and met American Indians who lived in the woodsy areas that surrounded Shadwell. The Jeffersons sometimes invited Cherokee leader Outacite and some of his people to visit them.

The Jeffersons owned lots of land—
and lots of slaves. In those days, plantation
farmers depended on African slaves to clear
the land, plow fields, and plant and harvest
crops. No one thought much about slaves'
rights in the 1700s. Plantation owners had
been forcing black slaves to work on their
plantations for years.

A cotton plantation in the South

Even though Thomas Jefferson owned slaves all his life, he knew it wasn't right. Thomas wrote a number of plans to stop or limit slavery. Slavery wasn't stopped, though, until years later, after the Civil War. Thomas Jefferson's ideas helped make the end of slavery finally possible.

When Thomas Jefferson was fourteen years old, his father died. Everyone was shocked because Mr. Jefferson had been known for his strength and energy. Being the oldest son in the family, Thomas inherited most of the plantation. At fourteen, he was suddenly very rich.

Thomas was ready to take charge of the plantation, but his mother told him that his father's last wish had been for Thomas to finish his schooling. Thomas followed his father's wishes. After finishing grade school, he entered William and Mary College in Williamsburg, Virginia.

Williamsburg was the capital of Virginia at the time. While at school there, Thomas attended parties where he met members of Virginia's government. Thomas became interested in how the government worked. He often went to government meetings and listened to important speakers there.

An engraving showing important buildings in Williamsburg in 1740

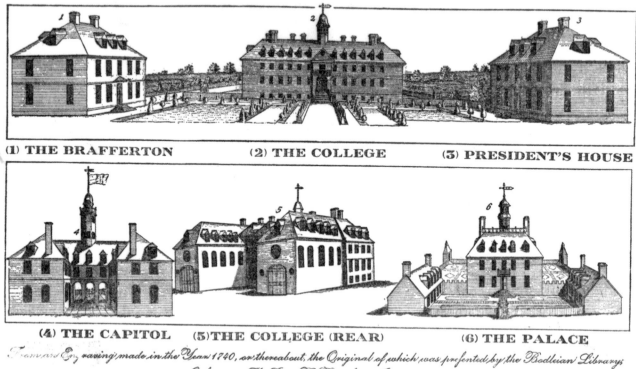

(1) THE BRAFFERTON   (2) THE COLLEGE   (3) PRESIDENT'S HOUSE

(4) THE CAPITOL   (5) THE COLLEGE (REAR)   (6) THE PALACE

From an Engraving made in the Year 1740, or thereabout, the Original of which was presented by the Bodleian Library, Oxford, to Mr. John D. Rockefeller, Jr., in 1937.

After he graduated from college, Thomas
became a successful lawyer. He spent his spare
time working on his new home at Monticello,
adding rooms and trying out new architectural
ideas. One night at a party, he met a girl named
Martha Skelton. Martha and Thomas got along
really well and ended up getting married in 1772.
Even though Thomas's house wasn't finished,
the newlywed couple moved in anyway.

As time went on, Thomas became more involved in the government of the Virginia Colony. He learned there were serious problems between the thirteen colonies and Great Britain. It seemed as if the king was always doing something to make people angry.

King George III made the colonists pay lots of extra taxes without giving them any say in the matter. Once, when the colonists refused to pay taxes on tea, King George closed down Boston's harbor as a punishment. He then sent British soldiers to keep an eye on the colonists and make sure they behaved themselves.

A portrait of King George III of England by Allan Ramsay (Blickling Hall, Norfolk, England)

At one government meeting, Thomas heard the patriot Patrick Henry make a speech. Patrick was fed up with England and the king. He said he would rather die than be treated unfairly by England. Patrick Henry's fiery speeches made lots of colonists want to rebel against England. Thomas Jefferson and others agreed. In 1775, some battles broke out between the colonists and British soldiers, touching off the Revolutionary War.

In 1776, Thomas Jefferson traveled to Philadelphia, Pennsylvania. He joined leaders from other colonies there at a meeting called the Continental Congress. This meeting was set up to discuss what the colonies were going to do about King George and the British government. The leaders of the colonies decided to break away from England. They asked George Washington to head up their army, and chose Thomas Jefferson to write a Declaration of Independence.

This painting by
J. L. G. Ferris shows
Thomas Jefferson
(at right) working
on the Declaration of
Independence with
Benjamin Franklin
(at left) and John Adams
(center).

Thomas Jefferson ended up writing one of
the most important historical documents ever.
He wanted the declaration to make it absolutely
clear why the colonies wanted to become their
own nation. His beautifully written document
is filled with ideas about rights and freedom
for all people. On July 4, 1776, the Declaration
of Independence was approved.

General Washington leading his soldiers during a Revolutionary War battle in 1777

As the Revolutionary War continued, Thomas Jefferson headed back to Virginia. In 1779, Thomas became the governor of Virginia. Even though it was a busy job, Thomas still found time to plant crops, work on his house, and read his favorite books.

While Thomas was governor, British soldiers attacked Virginia and caused a lot of damage. Thomas Jefferson was criticized for not spending enough time preparing for war and defending Virginia. Jefferson always felt he had let the people of Virginia down.

Finally, after six years of fighting, the Revolutionary War ended. The British gave up at Yorktown, Virginia, in 1781, and a peace treaty was signed in 1783.

After the war, Thomas Jefferson traveled to Paris, France, to join Benjamin Franklin and John Adams. These three patriots asked European countries for loans. They also worked out some business deals that would help the new United States of America.

Thomas enjoyed traveling all over Europe. He learned as much as he could about architecture, scientific discoveries, and new methods of farming. While in Italy, Thomas learned about a special type of rice. He thought this rice might grow well in the United States, but the Italian government said it would arrest anyone who tried to take rice out of Italy. Thomas Jefferson was so interested in the rice that he snuck some out of Italy anyway by stuffing it in his pockets!

A portrait of George Washington (known as the Landsdowne portrait) by Gilbert Stuart (National Portrait Gallery, Smithsonian Institution, Washington, D.C.)

In 1789, George Washington became the first president of the United States of America. He asked Thomas Jefferson to be one of his closest advisors. Even though Thomas Jefferson was itching to get back to Monticello to spend time farming, reading, and writing about his latest ideas, he accepted the position of secretary of state.

A portrait of Thomas Jefferson by Charles Willson Peale (the Huntington Library, Art Collections and Botanical Gardens, San Marino, California)

A portrait of John Adams by Bass Otis (New-York Historical Society, New York)

Thomas still felt bad about the job he had done as governor of Virginia. He thought that maybe he could make up for it by helping his new country get off to a good start.

Thomas Jefferson did an excellent job. A few years later, he became John Adams' vice president. Then, in 1800, Thomas Jefferson was elected third president of the United States.

The Rocky Mountains today

Thomas Jefferson was president for two terms, which is eight years. One lucky thing that happened while he was president was that he got the chance to buy the Louisiana Territory. This gigantic piece of land stretched all the way from the Mississippi River to the Rocky Mountains. It included the important city of New Orleans.

UNDER MY WINGS EVERY THING PROSPERS

An 1803 painting of the city and port of New Orleans by French artist
John L. Boqueta de Woiseri

Spain and then France had owned this territory. President Jefferson had been worried when France took it over. He knew that the French emperor, Napoleon Bonaparte, was interested in ruling the world. If Napoleon wanted to, he could cause a lot of problems for the new United States. For one thing, he controlled the busy shipping port of New Orleans.

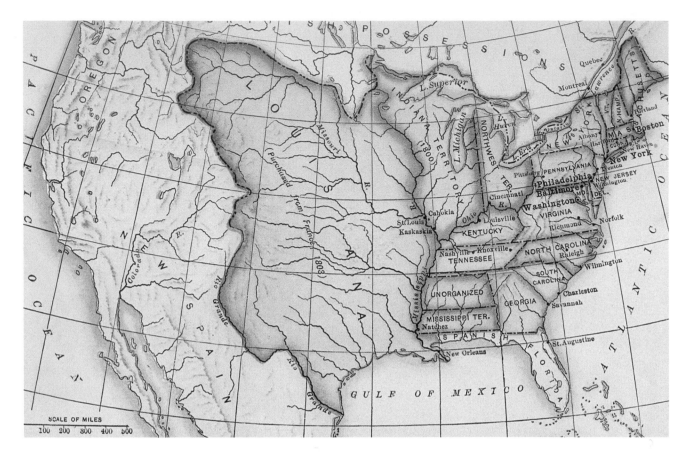

A map of the United States as it appeared in 1803

Thomas Jefferson decided to send a friend and advisor, James Monroe, to France to see if the United States might be able to buy New Orleans. James Monroe was surprised to discover that not only would Napoleon be happy to sell New Orleans, but he would throw in the whole Louisiana Territory for only $15 million.

Napoleon needed money right away to help pay for the wars his country was fighting. When Thomas Jefferson signed the agreement in 1803, he just about doubled the size of the United States.

An illustration showing Sacagawea, a Shoshone woman, guiding the Lewis and Clark Expedition through the Rocky Mountains

The Louisiana Territory was about 800,000 square miles (2,071,990 square kilometers) in size. There was a lot of unexplored land west of the Rocky Mountains, too. President Jefferson thought it would be a good idea to send someone to find out about the land that went all the way across North America to the Pacific Ocean.

These sketches from William Clark's diary show some of the wildlife Lewis and Clark saw during their expedition.

Jefferson asked Meriwether Lewis and William Clark to lead an expedition. In 1804, they headed west to explore unknown rivers and mountains.

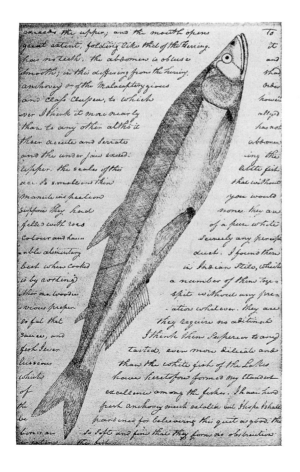

They were instructed to make friends with American Indians and learn about their customs. Lewis and Clark wrote lots of notes about the amazing things they saw.

A portrait of Thomas Jefferson at home at Monticello

Unfortunately, President Jefferson did have some problems he wasn't able to tackle. One of the biggest ones was that French and English navy ships began to stop American ships. They took cargo and kidnapped sailors for their own crew. Jefferson wasn't able to solve this problem and had to leave it for the next president to deal with.

When Thomas Jefferson finished his second term as president, he was happy to get back to Monticello. He spent his time coming up with important ideas about education and people's rights. He died on July 4, 1826, exactly fifty years after the Declaration of Independence was approved.